Text copyright © 2017 Juris Prudence LLC
Illustrations copyright © 2017 Juris Prudence LLC

All rights reserved. No parts of this book may be copied, reprinted, or otherwise reproduced in any matter without express written consent from the publisher.

The Juris Prudence & Associates Intern Case Kit is for fun, playful, and educational purposes only and is not intended to provide any legal advice or serve as actual legal documents.

ISBN-10: 1-946456-01-2
ISBN-13: 978-1-946456-01-4

Printed in the USA.

Juris Prudence LLC
www.jurispprudence.com

From the Desk of Juris P. Prudence

Hi Juris Prudence & Associates <u>**INTERN**</u>,

Thanks for interning with Juris Prudence & Associates! Maddy, Izzy, Sofie, and I are so happy that you have decided to join our team!

We think you are smart, dedicated, and responsible. We are leaving you with your own cases to take to <u>**COURT**</u>! Before <u>**COURT**</u>, take a look at the instructions behind this letter to learn how to use the Juris Prudence & Associates Case Kit.

All capitalized words in bold and underlined are vocabulary words, which are on the Vocabulary Sheet behind this letter. Study your vocabulary so that you can be a great <u>**INTERN**</u>!

Thanks for stepping in for Juris Prudence & Associates! Are you ready to make your case? Go for it!

Sincerely,

Juris P. Prudence :D

P.S. Remember, all items in this book are just for fun and are not real legal documents!

***Note to teachers and parents:

The Juris Prudence & Associates Intern Case Kit can be used in a variety of ways and for a variety of reasons, including the following:

Conflict resolution
Behavioral management
Persuasive writing skill development
Oral communication skill development
Creative writing skill development

Encourage students to use the Case Kit to advocate for issues that are important to them. A few fun topics to argue in 'court' are the following:

Should kids have a longer recess?
Should bedtime be longer?
Should kids be allowed to vote?
Should kids be able to drive at a younger age?
Should kids get an allowance?

JURIS PRUDENCE'S INTERN VOCABULARY

Clerk- Someone who works for a judge.

Contract- A written or oral agreement between two people or parties.

Court- A place where two or more people go to have a case heard in front of a judge or a jury.

Defendant- Someone who is defending himself or herself in a court. The defendant is the person who has allegedly done something wrong or bad, according to the plaintiff. This can be one person or a group of people.

Exhibit- Something a lawyer or party uses to help him or her support an argument or theory.

Intern- Someone who works for a trained person in order to learn a skill.

Judge- The person who makes a decision about the outcome of a case. A judge makes a ruling or decision in which he or she will agree or disagree with the parties in a case.

Jury- A group of people who make a decision about a case in court.

Law Firm- A business that is made up of one lawyer or a group of lawyers that work on legal cases.

Lawyer- Someone who has gone to law school, taken an exam called the bar exam, and gives advice about the law. Sometimes lawyers go to court, but not all lawyers go to court. Lawyers research, write, and communicate with others about the law. Lawyers are also called 'attorneys.'

Motion- A request before a judge to make a decision about an issue. A motion can be written down, made orally, or both.

Movant- The person who is asking a judge to do something. The movant uses a motion to make his or her request. This can be one person or a group of people.

Order- A judge's written or oral decision about a case.

Party- Someone appearing in front of a judge. A party can be a Plaintiff, Defendant, Movant, or Respondent.

Plaintiff- Someone who brings a case against another person. This can be one person or a group of people.

Respondent- The person is responding to the movant. This can be one person or a group of people. The respondent can respond to a motion orally, using a written opposition brief, or both.

Response- This is the written or oral communication from the Respondent about the Movant's Motion.

Ruling- A judge's decision on a party's case. The judge usually writes his or her ruling on something called an 'order.'

Subpoena- A document that tells the respondent the date, time, and place that the movant would like to argue his or her motion in front of the judge.

Vote- To choose between two or more people or things.

Witness- Someone who has seen or observed an event occur.

1) Study Your Vocabulary!

✓ Make sure you study the intern's vocabulary sheet in this book. It will define key words that you will need to know to be a great **INTERN**.

2) Gather your EXHIBITS!

✓ You may look for **EXHIBITS** from Internet sources and glue or tape them on your **EXHIBITS** page.

✓ You can also take pictures of **EXHIBITS** with your smart phone or tablet and print them out to put them on your **EXHIBITS** pages.

✓ If you can't find any pictures of **EXHIBITS**, write notes about incidents and things that you observe around you that you will use as **EXHIBITS** when arguing your motion. Take a look at the example **EXHIBITS** page.

3) Draft Your MOTION!

Have you decided which cases that you are going to take to **COURT**?

✓ If there is an issue that you think is important, you can make a **MOTION** to have that issue heard. For example, if you think your school recess should be longer, you can make a **MOTION** to extend the time for school recess. Take a look at the example **MOTION**!

✓ If you are making a motion or asking for something, you are called the **MOVANT**.

✓ The **MOVANT** has to write what he or she is requesting and the reason on his or her **MOTION**. For example, if the **MOVANT** believes that his or her school recess should be longer, the **MOVANT** has to use the **MOTION** to request this and explain why the **MOVANT** thinks that this should happen. Research reasons to support your motion, using books, newspapers, and the Internet. Interview witnesses who can provide statements to support your motion. When you write your motion, make sure you are answering the following questions: Who is affected by this motion? What is the purpose of the motion? Why should the judge grant the motion? How does the motion affect you? When should the judge's decision take effect?

4) Give your MOTION and SUBPOENA to the RESPONDENT!

✓ Give your **MOTION** to the **RESPONDENT**, and give them a **SUBPOENA**, which is a document that tells someone that they must attend court.

✓ The subpoena should tell the **RESPONDENT** the date, time, and place that the **MOVANT** would like to argue his or her motion in front of the **JUDGE**. Look at the example **SUBPOENA**!

5) Give the RESPONDENT a chance to respond to your MOTION!

✓ The **RESPONDENT** has to respond to the MOVANT's **MOTION**.

✓ If the **RESPONDENT** does not agree with the MOVANT's **MOTION**, the **RESPONDENT** has to write out his or her **RESPONSE**. For example, if the **RESPONDENT** does not believe that recess should be longer, the **RESPONDENT** must explain why on his or her **RESPONSE**. Look at the example **RESPONSE**!

6) Argue Your MOTION in Front of Your JUDGE!

✓ Once your **MOTION** is drafted, make your case in front of the **JUDGE**.

✓ Each **PARTY** must stand up and speak in front of the **JUDGE** about the **MOTION** and the **RESPONSE** to the **MOTION**. The **JUDGE** can be a parent, your teacher, a friend, or anyone else you choose. For this case kit, the **RESPONDENT** can also be the **JUDGE**.

✓ The **MOVANT** should first make his or her case in front of the **JUDGE**. Once the **MOVANT** has finished making his or her argument, the **RESPONDENT** has to respond to the MOVANT's **MOTION**.

✓ After the **RESPONDENT** has made his or her case, the **JUDGE** makes his or her decision and writes the decision down on his or her **ORDER**.

✓ The judge can grant (say yes to) or deny (say no to) the MOVANT's **MOTION**. Take a look at the example **ORDER**! The **JUDGE** should read his or her **ORDER** out loud.

EXAMPLE EXHIBIT

Playing outside makes kids HAPPY!

EXHIBIT 1

IN THE FICTICIOUS COURT
OF THE STATE OF JURISPRUDENCE

EXAMPLE MOTION

_____Madeline_____
MOVANT,

vs.   Case No. ___1234___

_____Madeline's Teacher_____
RESPONDENT(S).

MOVANT'S MOTION TO GET A LONGER RECESS

I move to get my class a longer recess because recess gives our class a chance to be outside and play. Our class needs more time for recess because the time that we have for recess now is very short. We don't have enough time to play games and talk to our friends on the playground. Being outside makes kids happy.

RESPECTFULLY SUBMITTED,
_____Madeline_____
MOVANT

EXAMPLE SUBPOENA

IN THE FICTICIOUS COURT
OF THE STATE OF JURISPRUDENCE

Madeline
_____
MOVANT,

Case No. ___1234____

v.s.

Madeline's Teacher
_____
RESPONDENT(S).

SUBPOENA TO APPEAR

I subpoena ___Madeline's Teacher_____ (Name of Respondent(s))

to appear at ___the Juris Prudence School___ . (Place)

on ___March 20, 2017 at 1:00 PM___ . (Date/Time)

RESPECTFULLY SUBMITTED,

Madeline
_____
NAME (Print Movant's Name(s))

EXAMPLE RESPONSE

IN THE FICTICIOUS COURT
OF THE STATE OF JURISPRUDENCE

_____Madeline_____
MOVANT,

vs.   Case No. __1234__

_____Madeline's Teacher_____
RESPONDENT(S).

RESPONSE TO MOVANT'S MOTION TO GET A LONGER RECESS

I respond to Movant's MOTION TO GET A LONGER RECESS by stating that I will consider granting this motion if Madeline and her class behave well this week. They must complete all homework assignments on time, behave in the classroom, and treat their classmates with respect and courtesy. If they do these things, I will grant them 10 extra minutes of recess on Friday.

RESPECTFULLY SUBMITTED,

_____Madeline's Teacher_____
RESPONDENT

EXAMPLE ORDER

IN THE FICTICIOUS COURT
OF THE STATE OF JURISPRUDENCE

_____
Madeline

MOVANT,

v.s.   Case No. _____ 1234

_____
Madeline's Teacher

RESPONDENT(S).

ORDER ON MOVANT's MOTION TO GET A LONGER RECESS

I rule that the Movant's Motion to Get a Longer Recess is GRANTED because MOVANT and her class have behaved excellently this week! Therefore, recess on Friday will be 10 minutes longer than usual.

SO ORDERED

_____
Madeline's Teacher
JUDGE

IN THE FICTICIOUS COURT
OF THE STATE OF JURISPRUDENCE

_____,

MOVANT,

vs.

_____ Case No. _____

RESPONDENT(S).

MOVANT'S MOTION TO _____

I move to _____
_____
_____
_____
_____
_____
_____
_____
_____
_____

RESPECTFULLY SUBMITTED,

_____
MOVANT

IN THE FICTICIOUS COURT
OF THE STATE OF JURISPRUDENCE

_____

MOVANT,

vs.   Case No. _____

_____

RESPONDENT(S).

SUBPOENA TO APPEAR

I subpoena _____ (Name of Respondent(s))

to appear at _____ (Place)

on _____ (Date/Time).

RESPECTFULLY SUBMITTED,

_____
NAME (Print Movant's Name(s))

IN THE FICTITIOUS COURT
OF THE STATE OF JURISPRUDENCE

_____,

MOVANT,

vs.   Case No. _____

_____,

RESPONDENT(S).

Response to Movant's Motion

I respond to Movant's Motion by stating _____
_____
_____
_____
_____
_____
_____
_____
_____

RESPECTFULLY SUBMITTED,

_____
RESPONDENT(S)

IN THE FICTITIOUS COURT
OF THE STATE OF JURISPRUDENCE

_____,

MOVANT,

vs.   Case No. _____

_____,

RESPONDENT(S).

ORDER ON _____

I rule that _____
_____
_____
_____
_____
_____
_____
_____
_____
_____

SO ORDERED,

_____
JUDGE

Witness Interview Notes

who? what? when? where? why? what if? How?

Case Notes

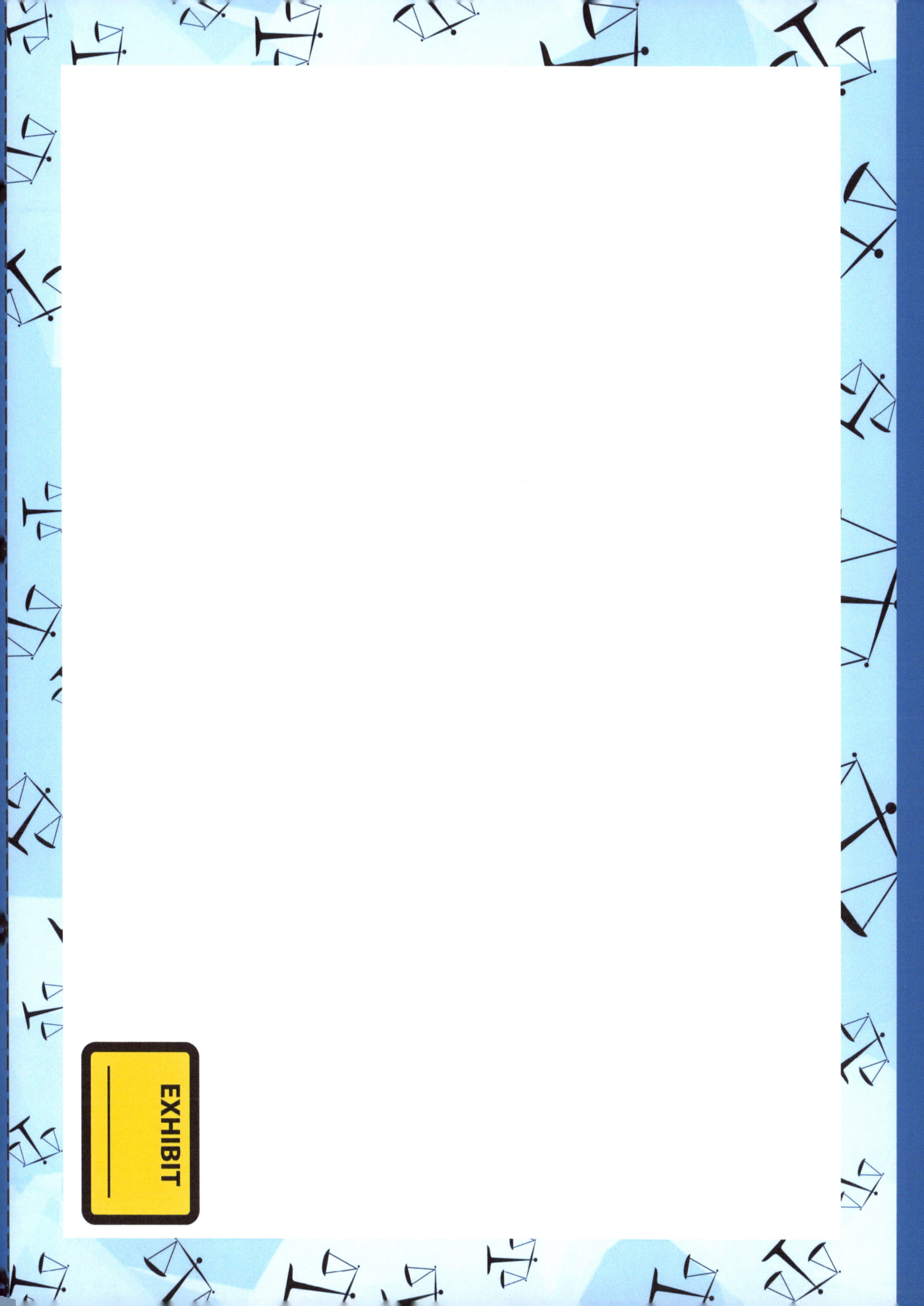

IN THE FICTICIOUS COURT
OF THE STATE OF JURISPRUDENCE

_____,

MOVANT,

vs.

_____, Case No. _____

RESPONDENT(S).

MOVANT'S MOTION TO _____

I move to _____
_____
_____
_____
_____
_____
_____
_____
_____
_____
_____

RESPECTFULLY SUBMITTED,

_____
MOVANT

IN THE FICTICIOUS COURT
OF THE STATE OF JURISPRUDENCE

_____

MOVANT,

vs. Case No. _____

_____

RESPONDENT(S).

SUBPOENA TO APPEAR

I subpoena _____ (Name of Respondent(s)

to appear at _____ (Place)

on _____ . (Date/Time)

RESPECTFULLY SUBMITTED,

_____

NAME (Print Movant's Name(s))

IN THE FICTITIOUS COURT
OF THE STATE OF JURISPRUDENCE

_____,

MOVANT,

vs.   Case No. _____

_____,

RESPONDENT(S).

Response to Movant's Motion

I respond to Movant's Motion by stating _____

_____

_____

_____

_____

_____

_____

_____

_____

_____

_____

RESPECTFULLY SUBMITTED,

_____

RESPONDENT(S)

IN THE FICTICIOUS COURT
OF THE STATE OF JURISPRUDENCE

_____,

MOVANT,

vs.   Case No. _____

_____,

RESPONDENT(S).

ORDER ON _____

I rule that _____

_____

_____

_____

_____

_____

_____

_____

_____

_____

_____

SO ORDERED,

_____
JUDGE

when? what? who?

Witness
Interview Notes

how? why? where?

Case Notes

IN THE FICTITIOUS COURT
OF THE STATE OF JURISPRUDENCE

_____,

    MOVANT,

vs.   Case No. _____

_____,

    RESPONDENT(S).

MOVANT'S MOTION TO _____

I move to _____

_____

_____

_____

_____

_____

_____

_____

RESPECTFULLY SUBMITTED,

_____

MOVANT

IN THE FICTICIOUS COURT
OF THE STATE OF JURISPRUDENCE

MOVANT,

vs.   Case No. _____

RESPONDENT(S).

SUBPOENA TO APPEAR

I subpoena _____ (Name of Respondent(s))

to appear at _____ (Place)

on _____ (Date/Time)

RESPECTFULLY SUBMITTED,

_____
NAME (Print Movant's Name(s))

IN THE FICTICIOUS COURT
OF THE STATE OF JURISPRUDENCE

_____

                    MOVANT,

vs.   Case No. _____

_____

                    RESPONDENT(S).

Response to Movant's Motion

I respond to Movant's Motion by stating _____
_____
_____
_____
_____
_____
_____
_____
_____

                    RESPECTFULLY SUBMITTED,

                    _____
                    RESPONDENT(S)

IN THE FICTITIOUS COURT
OF THE STATE OF JURISPRUDENCE

_____
)
)
MOVANT,   )
)   Case No. _____
vs.   )
)
_____)
)
RESPONDENT(S).   )

ORDER ON _____

I rule that _____

_____

_____

_____

_____

_____

_____

_____

_____

_____

SO ORDERED,

_____
JUDGE

Witness Interview Notes

who?? what?? when?? where?? why?? How??

Case Notes

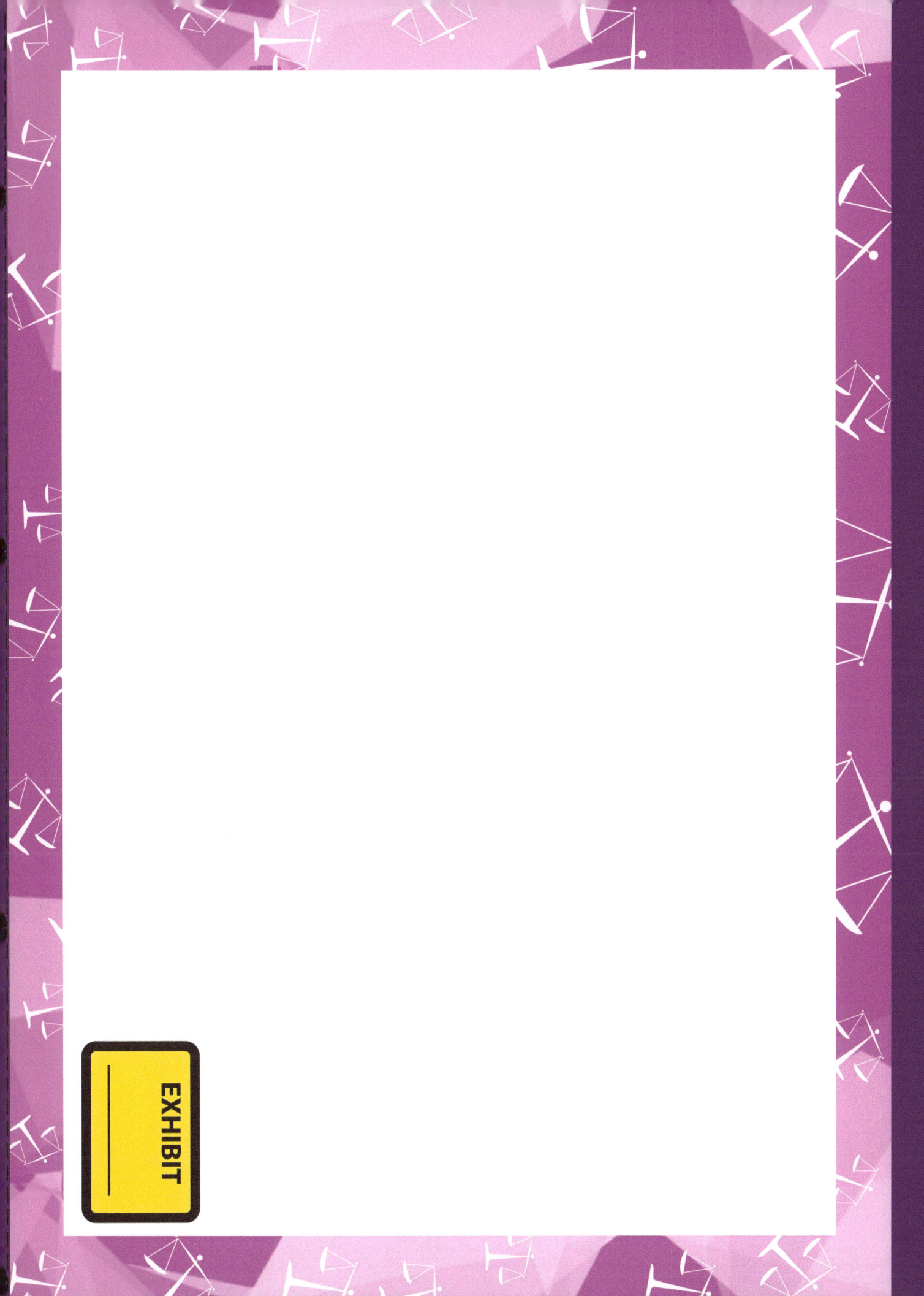

EXHIBIT ___

IN THE FICTICIOUS COURT
OF THE STATE OF JURISPRUDENCE

_____

MOVANT,

vs.

_____   Case No. _____

RESPONDENT(S).

MOVANT'S MOTION TO _____

I move to _____
_____
_____
_____
_____
_____
_____
_____
_____
_____
_____

RESPECTFULLY SUBMITTED,

_____
MOVANT

IN THE FICTICIOUS COURT
OF THE STATE OF JURISPRUDENCE

_____,

MOVANT,

vs.   Case No. _____

_____,

RESPONDENT(S).

SUBPOENA TO APPEAR

I subpoena _____ (Name of Respondent(s))

to appear at _____ (Place)

on _____ (Date/Time).

RESPECTFULLY SUBMITTED,

_____

NAME (Print Movant's Name(s))

IN THE FICTICIOUS COURT
OF THE STATE OF JURISPRUDENCE

_____,

MOVANT,

vs.   Case No. _____

_____,

RESPONDENT(S).

Response to Movant's Motion

I respond to Movant's Motion by stating _____

_____
_____
_____
_____
_____
_____
_____
_____
_____
_____

RESPECTFULLY SUBMITTED,

_____
RESPONDENT(S)

IN THE FICTICIOUS COURT
OF THE STATE OF JURISPRUDENCE

_____,

MOVANT,

vs.   Case No. _____

_____,

RESPONDENT(S).

ORDER ON _____

I rule that _____

_____

_____

_____

_____

_____

_____

_____

_____

SO ORDERED,

_____
JUDGE

who?

what?

when?

Interview Notes

Witness

how?

why?

where?

Case Notes

IN THE FICTITIOUS COURT
OF THE STATE OF JURISPRUDENCE

_____

MOVANT,

vs.   Case No. _____

_____

RESPONDENT(S).

MOVANT'S MOTION TO _____

I move to _____
_____
_____
_____
_____
_____
_____
_____
_____
_____
_____

RESPECTFULLY SUBMITTED,

_____
MOVANT

IN THE FICTICIOUS COURT OF THE STATE OF JURISPRUDENCE

_____

MOVANT,

vs.   Case No. _____

_____

RESPONDENT(S).

SUBPOENA TO APPEAR

I subpoena _____ (Name of Respondent(s))

to appear at _____ (Place)

on _____ (Date/Time)

RESPECTFULLY SUBMITTED,

_____
NAME (Print Movant's Name(s))

IN THE FICTITIOUS COURT
OF THE STATE OF JURISPRUDENCE

_____)
)
MOVANT,   )
)
vs.   )   Case No. _____
)
_____)
)
RESPONDENT(S).   )

Response to Movant's Motion

I respond to Movant's Motion by stating _____
_____
_____
_____
_____
_____
_____
_____
_____
_____

RESPECTFULLY SUBMITTED,

_____
RESPONDENT(S)

IN THE FICTITIOUS COURT
OF THE STATE OF JURISPRUDENCE

_____,

MOVANT,

vs.   Case No. _____

_____,

RESPONDENT(S).

ORDER ON _____

I rule that _____
_____
_____
_____
_____
_____
_____
_____
_____
_____

SO ORDERED,

_____
JUDGE

Witness Interview Notes

Who? What? When? Where? Why? How?

Case Notes

J.P.
Juris.Prudence

Juris Prudence awards this certificate to _____

for being a great Juris Prudence & Associates Intern.

— Juris P. Prudence

Date _____

www.ingramcontent.com/pod-product-compliance
Lightning Source LLC
Chambersburg PA
CBHW042017150426
43197CB00002B/60